SUMMERY OF THE SUMMER FRIEND
BY CHARLES MC Grath

Ronald A.Johnson

Table of content

Chapter 1

Chapter 2

Chapter 1

Sun-doused and significantly reaching.All along, the story's generally a grab sack. There's some stormy humanistic establishment about the democratization of diversion in America, followed by a faintly entertaining piece of family parentage that bets everything .

The veritable subject of The Summer Friend isn't playing golf or cruising or resting, or any of the other unwinding time practices that McGrath rhapsodizes about. As the title suggests, the center of the book is the story of a cooperation, and this is where it shines.

It's no spoiler to reveal that Chip G's. not great destruction makes a concealed region over the book. McGrath commends his pre-summer friend in unquestionably the initial segment, then, at that point, revives him on the resulting pages with such striking quality and clear love that the peruser neglects to recall his fate for huge length .

Exactly when the end finally comes, in a part fundamentally called 'Dying,' it lands like a stomach punch. Seeing Chip G is appalling. in his last days, and McGrath doesn't add to us the horrendous nuances.

Regretting his previous calm, he creates a letter to his dying buddy , endeavoring to offer his gratitude for their time together, yet at a similar time it's adequately not: 'This book is the very thing that I should have given him.'

McGrath's book is a showing of friendship, a fitting acknowledgment for his nearby pal and a strong idea to all of us to extricate every single drop from the summers that remain.

In these times of frantic journals, hard stories by overcomers of war and abuse, relocation and illness, is there a spot for a more settled white individual checking on splendid summers of golf and cruising.

I think there is, the place where it's created as cautiously as The Summer Friend, Charles McGrath's accolade for connection and contemplation McGrath's diary is as much about his young life summers everything being equal about his summers as a grown-up, and he moves forward and backward reliably between second individual (for the general) and first individual (for the specific).

That shift keeps the tone comfortable anyway, not dominatingly vain. These things I'm explaining, McGrath seems to say, are things we in general grasp .McGrath explains golf match-ups and floating excursions in perhaps more detail than most would have to examine, but the strength of the last areas is truly reaching.

Any person who has lost a buddy will fathom. affecting Mr. McGrath picks a confident , relaxed story tone that works without seeming to have anticipated his peruser.

It is watchfully acknowledged that the different activities
depicted are sufficiently interesting to arrange our
assent with no pressure on us to be fittingly shown in all
of them we can single out according as we would prefer.

I was a defective peruser of his longest segment,
'Destroying About in Boats,' since my life has been
spent without such destroying about, to be certain
practicing an uncommonly questionable association with
anything including significant water.

Regardless, Mr. McGrath's unpretentiousness is so
much that he makes no undertaking to convince us he's
participated in something we should proceed forward
with before it's too far to consider turning back.

Notwithstanding, he's restless to downplay the game
and his capacity in it .

The open doors for a solid story polishing off with death
are there, and Mr. McGrath makes plain how destroying
was the lack of his friend.

Notwithstanding, the other Chip, but routinely present
and dynamic in the story, isn't allowed to overwhelm it,
and until late leftover parts a steady, imaginative
accessory to the book's essential man, whether in
cruising or lobstering or golf.

This diary is tricky yet never makes over the moving
kinds of play it finds worth explaining ... The book's last
segment, 'Failing horrendously,' is a troublesome record
of Mr. McGrath's sidekick's passing, but the book's
general soul is totally strengthened .

It is in the finishing with which things enormous and little
are conveyed in the sum of their amusing identity that
spreads the word about what might be as the illustration
of the story that 'pre-summer can happen wherever.

Right when I was a young person, my family wasn't excited about get-aways. Cash was tight, and we by and large confined ourselves to travels, all of the five of us squeezed into a bubbling station truck vehicle A.C.

Why "the" instead of "my" buddy? Is it in light of the fact that "the" powers a particular significant distance, like the maker is suggesting a casual partner, while "my" addresses a closer relationship promising something more comfortable.

For this present circumstance, "the" seems to address the surface level of various male friendships diverged from the more significant bonds that women spread out.

The Summer Friend glimpses inside the brain of one such male partnership between not-precisely siblings unendingly yet periodic mates. In like manner, this diary is on the money for outdoorsy dads, kids, kin, uncles, nephews, and such.

McGrath, an award student at Yale (class of '68), high level as a man of letters, having been delegate editor of the New Yorker and a past boss of the New York Times Book Review. The present moment, he's boss of Golf Stories and a coincidental ally of Golf Digest.

Despite his academic certificates, there's a bit of whoopee cushion in the writer, who surveys with joy the cigarette load, a valuable joke contraption he and his kin implanted
into the tip of one of their mother's Old Gold cigarettes. Exactly when she enlightened, it exploded.

"Eccentric, I know," creates McGrath, as of now 76, "but the memory of my mother staying there, wide-checked out, with an exploded cigarette in her mouth really causes me to obliterate with laughing."

Obviously, the prankster grew up to value fireworks; even today, as a granddad, he consumes numerous dollars on July Fourth celebrations, where he shoots off

poppers, rockets, salutes, and wafers by the block and half-block.
Truly, he gives an entire part to "Detonating Stuff.

The part that most describes McGrath, in any case, is "The Camp," and his memories of the long get-aways his family took to the kind of log-created stop normal to various families the country over back then.

For the McGraths, it was "a short sun-dappled idyll, a concise glance at another kind of life," where kids bought penny candy, red hots and little wax suppresses stacked with sweet, sweet liquid.

"A piece of what made the Camp basic to every one of us even to my mother — was that it was a traction on uniqueness, a perch on the regular workers, where we genuinely ought not be having a spot. People like us didn't have summer places. None of our neighbors at home did.

Encountering adolescence during the 1950s with little golf, drive-in movies, and amplified vehicles, McGrath learned about sex from tuning in on "hot rodders" playing under their rides.

I contemplated that sex, like experts, ought to be generally an issue of expertise. You expected to grasp what occurred in the motor."

Right now, you've tracked down that this journal is more about the author than his subject, and parts are horrendously hopeless, particularly when McGrath clarifies his people.

His mother, who married under her cultural position, appears to have been exorbitantly appended to Manhattanites and once in a while criticized his father for his deficiencies.

Social class and [his] lack as a provider were consistent subjects in my people's marriage."

It was an inclination shared by McGrath himself.
Recollecting, he regrets that his father died "before we
could move past being unsettled in each other.

He fantasizes about grabbing his dad's arm and going
for a sail, which is reminiscent of "Divine area," the film
about a kid baseball field and seats to reconnect with
his father: "Build it and they will come.

Here enters the other Chip, the brilliant summer buddy
who will not at any point disappoint. Together, the two
men while away their days raising a ruckus around town
and fishing and cruising.

They make standard trips to the landfill to look for
discarded clubs; in the evenings, they barbecue and
drink "brewskis" with their life partners. In 30 years,
there won't ever be a cross word between them.

McGrath goes long and significant on cruising and gives pages to his valued Beetle, the last productively fabricated wooden boat really being sold in America.

"The joy of this never gets old for me," he communicates, "the shiver of the sail, the slap of the bow wave, the burbling of the wake, the draw of the turner, the lift of the brutal quarter as it gets a swell."

The nuances of cruising are different, fascinating even, but he also waxes lovely about birds:

Gulls everywhere; the cormorants waiting, shrug-bore, on rocks and pilings; and the egrets, which perch unmoving in trees when they're not mincing through the shallows."

McGrath plainly recollects, also, the days he and Chip would meet first thing, pulling their used clubs, and drive to five exceptional courses to play 90 openings of golf by 9 p.m., when it was excessively dull to try and think about continuing.

They did this in shoes since they considered spikes a
motion. The maker contemplates these excursions with
the pride of Hannibal crossing the Alps with 37
elephants.

Nevertheless, individual nuances of his association? Not
actually. "Perhaps [Chip] had inside him a massive
storm cellar where he could drive away a large number
of stresses and bothers," McGrath makes. "I'm not much
better.

Chapter 2

Regardless, when Chip is passing on from dangerous
development, all through clinical facilities, unsuitable to
walk, committed to using a stick, then, a walker, in
conclusion incontinent and attached to a bed

nevertheless, by the day's end the two men examine the environment and the opportunities for the Red Sox.

Moving right along before Chip passes on, McGrath shows up inside himself and makes a letter, saying curiously how much their bond has inferred.

I said he was what Romantics used to call a virtuoso loci — the spirit of a spot, its epitome in an individual… I recorded things I had been expecting to say for a seriously prolonged stretch of time… it was too far to turn back.

Likewise, I probably don't express anything near anything. This book is the very thing that I should have given him."

Corporations are a key fixing in an euphoric life. This is the method for offering them enough thought and thought.

How might one make huge connections and relationships as an adult? The following are a couple of thoughts and important instruments.

The pandemic has made everything harder, including making new partners. However, it can in like manner be an opportunity to be more purposeful about the ones we keep.

All associations require some work. For your friendships to thrive, base on your abilities to listen, sympathy and correspondence.

It's exceptionally typical for people to feel want or desire toward their sidekicks. Luckily, there are approaches to changing those sentiments into fostering an entryway.

Being an old amigo suggests offering your assistance amidst difficulty. Essentially recall: Sometimes less is better than more.

In these times of basic journals hard stories by overcomers of war and abuse, relocation and sickness is there a spot for a more settled white individual exploring splendid summers of golf and floating.I think there is a place where it's made as delicately as "The Summer Friend," Charles McGrath's recognition for friendship and contemplation.

The buddy in the title is Chip Gillespie, an individual McGrath (generally called Chip) meets one summer when their youngsters are at this point energetic.

The McGrath family rents a sea side house in the Massachusetts town where Gillespie and his better half live. The two couples meet at a square dance, "for the wellbeing of goodness," McGrath creates, and find they share a ton basically .

notwithstanding a comparative moniker, but a veneration for cruising, youngsters named Ben, young ladies a comparable age. Starting there springs a well established cooperation that has out for the most influence throughout the span of the significant stretches of summer.

McGrath's diary is as much about his young life summers in every way that really matters, about his summers as a grown-up, and he moves back and forth faultlessly between second individual (for the general) and first individual (for the specific).

That shift keeps the tone individual yet not prevalently self-absorbed. These things I'm clarifying, McGrath seems to say, are things we overall fathom.

What actuated the diary, clearly, was Chip's death. While the end is referred to only tenderly for a huge piece of the book, it looms over the euphoric sundrenched segments, giving them weight.

McGrath explains golf match-ups and cruising trips in perhaps more detail than most would have to scrutinize, but the force of the last segments is genuinely reaching. Any person who has lost a friend will fathom.

The title of Charles McGrath's impacting diary suggests a man, by and by dead, with whom Mr. McGrath had a significant friendship and shared the moniker "Chip.

 What they in like manner shared, even more in a general sense, was an overflow of New England summer practices resolved to delight: from golf, swimming and boat running to Fourth of July fireworks and lobstering.

Chip McGrath's working life included changing and making for the New Yorker and the New York Times Book Review; his life of play was the area, beginning with youthfulness, when summer mid year — gave substance and greatness to everything aside from work.

the time, in Mr. McGrath's words, when there was "with parts yet inactive time, yet there was nothing you ought to do." Summer's presence itself is the "buddy" who made possible the things that significantly matter.

Mr. McGrath, by and by 74 and a contributing writer at the Times, picks a private, relaxed story tone that works without seeming to have anticipated his peruser.

It is cautiously expected that the different activities depicted are sufficiently interesting to arrange our assent with no stress on us to be suitably shown in all of them we can single out as we would prefer.

I was a defective peruser of his longest segment, "Destroying About in Boats," since my life has been spent without such destroying about, to be certain practicing an extraordinarily questionable association with anything including significant water.

20

However, Mr. McGrath's unpretentiousness is somuch
that he makes no undertaking to convince us he's
participated in something we should move forward with
before it's too far to consider turning back. In any case,
he's restless to downplay the game and his ability in it.

A long cooperation blends a consideration of
pre-summer in this sensitive commemoration.

New York Times creator McGrath gets back to
hismasculine relationship with Chip Gillespie, a modeler
who dwelled in the little Massachusetts town where
McGrath and his family went from here onward,
indefinitely quite a while the relationship included a great
deal cruising.

significant distance race rounds of golf, playing
misrepresentations at parties, lighting firecrackers, and
imprudent breeze shooting (Q. "If you were sitting tight
for the death penalty, what could you want as your last
blowout?.

In any event, probably not going to need to eat").He twists in various recollections: youth idylls at his people's cabin; breaking into deserted Yale structures with his better half, Nancy; going to the town dump; ultimately, watching Chip give up to illness.

McGrath's piece unspools like a long summer day,stacked with ventures that set out in questionable direction and appear at brilliant spots spilling over with rich sensations (On jumping off an expansion into a stream.

That long depiction of quick drop is both exciting and heart-thumpingly frightening, and when.you traverse the surface, taking in an exceptional, leaned toward breath of air, the tendency is one of mind boggling help.

Through his sparkling, survey point ofconvergence, McGrath gets life at its by and large cheerful and critical. thoughtfully considers New England trips and an interesting adult connection.

He twists around together three separate strands of memories: vivacious summers at his family's retreat, "a spot we called the Camp"; summers with his soul mate and children ("it's plausible to be depleted half insane yet have an extremely extraordinary time"); and summers with Chip and his family, whom they met a lengthy move away.

Memories thrive, as one prompts another, then, at that point, another, floating truly changing in time.

The maker surveys the fervor of framework bouncing into water 30 feet down; making fireworks runs and lighting them on the fourth of July; and "destroying about in boats" of various kinds, especially his father's dearest Chris-Craft runabout made of mahogany wood," which "was so wonderfully finished that, out of the water, it was by all accounts a family thing.

Chip, a superb sailor, told McGrath the best way tovoyage, and the maker appreciates explicitly depicting those endeavors.

He moreover lovingly accounts his different summer homes, including Snowdie and its 62 seats; Chip's family home that the McGraths rented; and their own revered 1930s Cape with its mid year house various things.

The story expects a self-goal against the character
when the maker sorts out that his 57-year-close pal has
prostate dangerous development.

They had a go at hanging out as the infection spread.
McGrath recollects about the "companionship of normal
point of view" while lobstering, the two families
swimming together, and when he and Chip played golf,
chuckling at each other's dreadful shots.

Sadly, Chip passed on in 2015. "I wish we had the
conversation" about his approaching death, creates
McGrath, "to ultimately benefit my own, despite his." He
wishes he had said more. "This book," he notes, "is
what I should have given him."

Everyone needs power and everyone is in a consistent
misdirecting game to obtain capacity to the burden of
others, according to Greene, a screenwriter and past
manager at Esquire (Elffers, a book packager, arranged
the volume, with its charming marginalia).

We live today as subjects once did in majestic courts:
we ought to appear to be normal while trying to crush all
of the individuals around us.
This power game can be played well or ineffectually, and
in these 48 guidelines isolated from the arrangement of
encounters and quickness of the world's most
imperative power players are the rules that ought to be
adhered to win.

These guidelines decrease to being as hardhearted,
narcissistic, manipulative, and insidious as could be
anticipated. Each guideline, anyway, gets its own part.

Conceal Your Intentions," "Reliably Say Less Than
Necessary," "Stance as a Friend, Work as a Spy, and so
forth. Each part is supportively isolated into regions on
what came upon individuals who abused or saw the
particular guideline, the basic parts in this guideline, and
ways to deal with defensively switching this guideline
when it's used against you.

References in the edges improve the model being taught. While persuading in the way an auto crash might be, the book is essentially trash.

Oversees much of the time conflict with each other. We are told, for instance, to "be unmistakable at all cost," then, at that point, told to "carry on like others." More really, Greene never genuinely portrays "power," and he essentially states, instead of offering confirmation for, the Hobbesian universe of all against all where he requests we live.

The world may resemble this every so often, yet habitually it isn't. To ask concerning why this is so would be an unquestionably more supportive errand.

He was the only one of the family to persevere through what Francois Maurois, in his show, calls the "human holocaust" of the abuse of the Jews, what began with the restrictions, the singularization of the yellow star, the separated region inside the ghetto, and happened to the mass removals to the grills of Auschwitz and Buchenwald.

There are wonderful and shocking scenes here in this extra and troubling diary of this experience of the hanging of a youngster, of his most significant farewell with his father who leaves him a tradition of a sharp edge and a spoon, and of his last goodbye at Buchenwald his father's body is at this point cool also the extensive stretches of perseverance under improper conditions.

"To lose yourself in your own past summers, especially the ones of your experience growing up, when you imagined there'd be a boundless number of them, and moreover allies to give those summers to.

That both turn out to be numbered makes this book vehemently hurt with greatness and hardship."

It was evening and one more partner had come to recuperate his young lady from a play date. As opposed to driving up in a minivan, he appeared by water, joining his boat shrewdly across a squiggly channel might you eventually go against getting to realize a man like that?

All through the range of this rich diary, McGrath surveys with a drill eye the pleasures of summers past: beginner lobstering, 9-opening golf, family troupe misrepresentations, length bouncing, and a friendship molded between two men from different establishments who got together late all through regular daily existence.

Depicting the whims of summer with such precision and warmth- - stripping long bits consumed by the sun skin from your shoulder like "revamping off your own cover," the external shower conceal blowing open in the breeze, a M80 firework in the letter drop .

The Summer Friend is simultaneously a strong calling of the rhythms and

Furthermore , functions of summer and a mixing acknowledgment of a sidekick saw as and thereafter lost.

In these times of frantic journals — hard accounts of
overcomers of war and abuse, relocation and sickness
— is there a spot for a more established white man who
reviews splendid summers of golf and floating? I think
when it's formed as delicately as "The Summer Friend,"
there's Charles McGrath's accolade for cooperation and
contemplation.

The buddy in the title is Chip Gillespie, a youngster who
McGrath (also called Chip) meets one summer when
their young people are at this point energetic.

The McGrath family rents a sea side house in the town
of Massachusetts, where Gillespie and his soulmate
live.

The two couples meet during a square dance, "for the
wellbeing of goodness," makes McGrath, and find they
share a ton for all plans and reason notwithstanding a
comparative moniker, yet a love for cruising, kids named
Ben, young ladies of a comparable age.

Starting there a well established friendship cultivates
that fundamentally occurs in the mid year months.

McGrath's diary is as much about the summers of his life as a young person as he is about his summers as an adult, moving perfectly between second individual (for the general) and first individual (for the specific).

That shift keeps the tone individual, yet totally not dominatingly egocentric. These things that I explain, McGrath is apparently saying, are things that we in general understand.

The trigger for the diary was, clearly, Chip's passing. While death is only delicately referred to for a critical piece of the book, it looms over the ecstatic, sun-doused segments, giving them weight.

McGrath clarifies golf match-ups and boat trips in perhaps more detail than most should examine, but the effect of the last parts is truly moving. Any person who has lost a buddy will come

9 798838 090461